D0859458

**DATE DUE**

Metro Litho
Oak Forest, IL 60452

| | | | |
|---|---|---|---|
| | | | |
| | | | |
| | | | |
| | | | |
| | | | |
| | | | |
| | | | |
| | | | |
| | | | |
| | | | |
| | | | |
| | | | |
| | | | |

111906

08047-4

796.334   Howard, Dale E
HOW     Soccer stars

DISCARD

LIBRARY
TELLURIDE PUBLIC SCHOOLS
TELLURIDE, COLORADO 81435

# Soccer Stars

**Dale E. Howard**

111906

## CHILDRENS PRESS®

CHICAGO

## Dedication

To my son, Damon

## Photo Credits

cover: ©Mitchell B. Reibel/Sports Photo Masters, Inc.; page 1, Shaun Botterill/ ©Allsport; 3, ©Popperfoto; 5, Allsport/Pressens Bild; 6, ©Allsport; 9, 10 (both photos), 11 (all photos), 12, 13, AP/Wide World; 14, 15, 16, ©Popperfoto; 17, UPI/Bettmann; 18, 20, ©Popperfoto; 21, Jonny Graan/Allsport/©Pressens Bild AB; 22, Allsport/©Pressens Bild; 23, 25 (bottom), UPI/Bettmann; 25 (top), ©Allsport; 26 ©Popperfoto; 28, Focus on Sports; 29, ©Mitchell B. Reibel/Sports Photo Masters, Inc.; 30, Bob Thomas Sports Photography; 31, AP/Wide World; 32, UPI/Bettmann; 33 (top), ©Allsport 33 (bottom), The Bettmann Archive; 34, AP/Wide World; 35, UPI/Bettmann; 36, ©Horst Müller; 37, Bob Thomas Sports Photography; 39, ©Horst Müller; 40, 41, AP/Wide World; 42, Bob Thomas Sports Photography; 44, Reuters/Bettmann; 45, UPI/Bettmann; 47, ©Allsport

## Editorial Staff

*Project Editor:* Mark Friedman
*Design and Electronic Composition:* TJS Design
*Photo Editor:* Jan Izzo

## Library of Congress Cataloging-in-Publication Data

Howard, Dale E.
Soccer stars / by Dale E. Howard.
p. cm. — (World Cup soccer)  Includes index.
ISBN 0-516-08047-4
1. Soccer players—Biography—Juvenile literature. [1. Soccer players.]
I. Title. II. Series.

GV939.A1H69  1994                                          93-44458
796.334'092'2—dc20                                              CIP
[B]                                                              AC

©1994 by Childrens Press®, Inc.
All rights reserved. Published simultaneously in Canada.
Printed in the United States of America
    2 3 4 5 6 7 8 9 10 R 03 02 01 00 99 98 97 96 95 94

# Table of Contents

# Introduction

Every sport has one player who outshines all the others. You can't think about basketball without thinking of Michael Jordan—but very soon you also think of Charles Barkley, Larry Bird, and Magic Johnson.

If someone asks you who the greatest ice hockey player is, you probably say, "Wayne Gretzky." But older people may also think about Bobby Hull, Bobby Orr, or Maurice Richards.

And who's the best baseball player of all time? Babe Ruth immediately comes to mind. But what about Hank Aaron, who broke Ruth's home run record, or pitchers like Nolan Ryan, Sandy Koufax, and Cy Young?

## Who's really the best?

The same debates are argued about soccer. When you talk about soccer stars, people think first of Pelé, who did things with a soccer ball few others

dream of. But Artur Friedenreich actually scored
more goals, and Stanley Matthews played much
longer. And then you have to consider great
goalies like Lev Yashin and Gordon Banks.

This book tells the stories of ten of the best soccer
players the world has ever seen. There were many
others who could have been included.

You are probably familiar with baseball, basketball,
and American football. But soccer is the world's
game. Did you know that in most countries soccer
is called "football"? Listed on the next two pages
are some terms used in this book you may not know.

# Dictionary of World Soccer

### back (or deep back)

A defensive player who is positioned in front of the goalie and goal.

### clubs

Soccer teams are called clubs in most parts of the world. They are traditionally a part of larger social organizations.

### European Cup

The European Champion Clubs' Cup is the top championship for Europe's professional soccer clubs.

### European Footballer of the Year

The highest honor given to a professional soccer player in Europe. This award is made by the French magazine *France Football.*

### FIFA

Stands for *Fédération Internationale de Football Association,* or the International Federation of Football Associations. FIFA is the organization that governs professional soccer, keeps world records, and runs the World Cup.

**The Football Association**

The first soccer association, founded in England in 1863. The word "soccer" comes from shortening the word "association." The F.A. Cup (Football Association Cup) is England's professional championship.

**forward**

A player who plays at the front of his or her team, usually in an attacking position.

**goalkeeper (goalie)**

Guards the goal and the area around the goal. Only the goalkeeper may touch the ball with his or her hands.

**midfielder**

Plays in the middle of the field, between the forwards and the backs.

**North American Soccer League (NASL)**

The leading professional soccer league in the United States from 1968 until 1984. The NASL hired stars from all over the world to play in America.

**striker**

A forward whose job is to score goals.

**wing (winger)**

Plays near the sidelines of a soccer field. A team can have a left and a right winger. They often dribble the ball up the sidelines and then kick a pass to teammates near the goal.

**World Cup**

The international soccer championship between the countries of the world. The tournament is held once every four years.

# Artur Friedenreich

*Artur was Brazil's first superstar. He thrilled soccer fans with brilliant plays. He was a master of deception and trick shots. He faked out goalkeepers, seeming to score a goal whenever he wanted one. And he scored more goals than anyone else in history.*

**A**rtur Friedenreich was the son of a German father and a black Brazilian mother. He was one of the first nonwhites to play with Brazil's best teams. This helped open Brazilian soccer to black and racially mixed fans and players.

Artur played most of his games for clubs around his hometown of São Paulo. The best club was named Paulistano. Artur helped his teams win ten Brazilian championships.

He also appeared 22 times for his country, Brazil, in international competition. He led the South American championship teams in 1919 and 1922.

BRAZIL

He played his best soccer during these championships. His amazing footwork and ball control delighted fans all over South America. Argentines called him *el Tigre,* the tiger, for the way he seemed to pounce on the ball and outrun his opponents.

In 1925, Artur led Paulistano, his Brazilian club team, on a thrilling tour of Europe. His fame spread around the world.

Ten years later, Artur ended his career at age 43. He scored more goals than anyone else in world soccer history. The FIFA officially credits him with 1,329 goals in senior competition. Only two other players—Pelé and Austria's Franz Binder—have scored more than 1,000 goals in their careers.

To this day, some Brazilian soccer fans still say that Artur was the best player ever—better than all who followed.

**Born**
1892

**Died**
1969

**Country**
Brazil

**Position**
Forward

# Sports World Leaders

Artur Friedenreich

*Artur Friedenreich scored more goals than any other soccer player in world history. Here are the all-time worldwide kings in several sports.*

| SOCCER | Goals |
|---|---|
| 1. Artur Friedenreich, Brazil, 1909–35 | 1,329 |
| 2. Pelé, Brazil, 1956–77 | 1,280 |
| 3. Franz Binder, Austria, 1930–50 | 1,006 |

| BASEBALL | Home Runs |
|---|---|
| 1. Sadurahu Oh, Japan, 1959–80 | 868 |
| 2. Henry Aaron, U.S., 1954–76 | 755 |
| 3. Babe Ruth, U.S., 1914–35 | 714 |

Sadurahu Oh

| FOOTBALL | Rushing Yards |
|---|---|
| 1. Walter Payton, U.S., 1975–87 | 16,726 |
| 2. Eric Dickerson, U.S., 1983–93 | 13,168 |
| 3. Tony Dorsett, U.S., 1977–88 | 12,739 |

Left to right: Gordie Howe,
Walter Payton and
Kareem Abdul-Jabbar

## BASKETBALL

| | Points |
|---|---|
| 1. Kareem Abdul-Jabbar, U.S., 1969–89 | 38,387 |
| 2. Wilt Chamberlin, U.S., 1954–73 | 31,419 |
| 3. Julius Erving, U.S., 1972–87 | 30,026 |

## HOCKEY

| | Goals |
|---|---|
| 1. Gordie Howe, U.S., 1946–71, 1979–80 | 801 |
| 2. Wayne Gretzky, Canada/U.S., 1978– | 764* |
| 3. Marcel Dionne, U.S., 1971–89 | 731 |

*thru 1993 season

# Sir Stanley Matthews

**Born**
1915

**Country**
England

**Position**
Right Wing

ENGLAND

*Matthews faked and dribbled around opposing backs almost at will, setting up goals for teammates with superb passes.*

Stanley Matthews was the greatest English star. He played professional soccer for more than 30 years, until he was 50 years old. In 1956, he won the first European Footballer of the Year award. In 1965, he became the only soccer player knighted by an English monarch.

Stanley was a right winger. He earned the name "Wizard of Dribble" for his amazing ball control. He faked and dribbled around opposing backs almost at will, setting up goals for teammates with superb passes.

Stanley himself scored "only" 71 goals in 698 games. Still, he controlled the games he played. And he scored several important goals that will be remembered for generations.

Perhaps his best goal was the winner in the 1953 English F.A. Cup. Stanley's team, Blackpool, trailed

Bolton 1-3 with about 23 minutes left in the game. Even when one of Stanley's teammates, Mortensen, hit a goal, the score was still 2-3 and Blackpool seemed doomed to lose.

Then, with only three minutes left, Stanley kicked one of his great passes high across the Bolton goal. Mortensen was there. He drove the ball into the Bolton net, tying the game at 3-3.

Matthews meets England's King George VI in 1948.

Stanley then won the game on his own. The final minute of the game is known as the "Stanley Matthews Minute." He dribbled up the right sideline, faking out several defenders as he went. He passed the ball to *himself* through the legs of a defender! No one could stop him.

Matthews dribbles past a
stunned defender.

With seconds ticking away, he positioned himself to
pass to Mortenson across the goal. As he went to
kick the ball, his foot caught in the grass, spraining
his ankle. As he was still in motion, he decided he
should shoot rather than pass. He twisted his body
and shot for the Bolton goal. As he collapsed to
the ground in pain, Stanley heard the crowd roar
as his winning goal went in.

# Alfredo di Stefano Lauthe

**Born**
1926

**Country**
Argentina

**Position**
Center Forward

*Di Stefano played all over the center of the field. His great energy, superb ball control, and powerful shots enabled him to direct his teammates and dominate games.*

ARGENTINA

As the center forward of Spain's Real Madrid soccer club, di Stefano dominated European football. He led his team to a record six European Cups. His 49 goals in European Cup games is a record that still stands. In his entire career, he scored more than 800 goals, leading the Spanish league in scoring five times. He was twice named European Footballer of the Year.

Alfredo was born in Argentina, but his family was Italian. He developed a powerful body at a young age and maintained top physical condition throughout his career. Because he was right-footed, his father made him shoot only with his left foot when he was a boy. This helped Alfredo develop the ability to dribble and score with either foot.

Alfredo began playing professional soccer with an Argentine team called River Plate. He soon became

Di Stefano shoots for a goal.

Argentina's top goal scorer. In one 66-game season he scored 50 times! He was selected for the national team seven times and became famous everywhere in South America.

In 1949, di Stefano moved to Colombia, where he scored 259 goals in 292 games for his new team. He also led his team to two Colombian championships and played four times for Colombia's national team.

Continuing his travels, di Stefano moved to Spain in 1953. He played for Real Madrid and soon made it the best club team ever. Di Stefano played all over the center of the field. His great energy, superb ball control, and powerful shots enabled him to direct his teammates and dominate games.

When the great Hungarian Ferenc Puskás joined him as the left forward, the Real Madrid front line was unstoppable. In nine years with Real Madrid, di Stefano scored 405 goals in 624 games. At the same time, Puskás led the Spanish league in scoring four times.

During this time, di Stefano became a Spanish citizen and played on Spain's national team (the third country he played for). After retiring as a player, di Stefano helped manage teams in Argentina and in Spain. In both countries he turned losing teams into winners.

No matter what he did, Alfredo di Stefano was a champion.

# Lev Yashin

**Born**
1929

**Country**
Russia

**Position**
Goalkeeper

*Yashin would often emerge from a pile of fallen players with the ball in his arms and a smile on his face.*

RUSSIA

Lev Yashin is called soccer's greatest goalie because of his acrobatic saves and safe goalkeeping. He was the most famous Russian star, and he gave his teammates confidence. In any situation, they knew they could rely on him.

A tall, lanky man with long arms, Lev controlled the penalty area around his own goal. He challenged opposing players who approached, coming out from his goal to dive for the ball. He would often emerge from a pile of fallen players with the ball in his arms and a smile on his face. Sometimes he would jokingly shake his finger at an opponent who had just tried—and failed—to score against him.

Lev began playing professional soccer in 1953 for a team called Dynamo Moscow. It would be his only club, and he played more than 600 games for it. Dynamo won five Russian championships and two

A familiar sight: Yashin diving for a save

professional cups with Lev in the goal. "The Man in Black" (Lev always wore black when in goal) became famous all over the world for his sportsmanship and good humor. He was loved even by fans of opposing teams.

Lev anchored Russia's 1956 Olympic gold-medal team. He also led Russia to three World Cup tournaments and the first European Nation's Cup championship, in 1960.

In 1971, Lev played his last game, a special testimonial game just for him. Stars came from all over the world to play against Dynamo and salute the great Lev Yashin.

# Gordon Banks

**Born**
1937

**Country**
England

**Position**
Goalkeeper

*He was strong, he played with courage, and he protected the goal with catlike acrobatic moves. Gordon Banks was the best English goalkeeper ever, only the second goalie to be named England's Player of the Year (in 1972).*

He developed his talent through hours of hard practices and studying film of himself and other goalies. His pregame stretching routine was legendary. So was the way he talked to himself during games.

Gordon appeared on two of England's World Cup teams. He was the hero of their 1966 World Cup championship. He allowed only three goals in the six final games!

He also dazzled opponents in the 1970 World Cup. Perhaps the finest save of his career came against Brazil in 1970. Brazilian forward Jairzinho raced down the right side, dribbling the ball ahead of him.

Suddenly he kicked the ball high across the goal. The great Pelé raced to the goal, leaped, and headed the ball down toward the corner. He waved his hands triumphantly and shouted "Goal!" But Gordon, diving full length, reached out and tipped the ball over the crossbar.

Banks (right), defends the goal in the 1966 World Cup.

A spectacular Banks save!

Pelé called Gordon's save "spectacular... impossible," the greatest he had ever seen. Gordon admitted it was the best save of his career, but he had other great ones as well.

In 1972, Gordon led his club team, Stoke, to its first English League Cup by saving a penalty shot. Penalty shots almost always result in goals. The ball

is placed directly in front of the goal, and the player taking the shot runs to the ball and usually kicks it toward a corner. The goalkeeper must stay on his own goal line and not move his feet until the ball is kicked. The goalie usually guesses which direction to dive. Even if he guesses right, it's difficult to stop the shot.

Gordon's great 1972 penalty save came in a semifinal game, with three minutes to go in overtime. He had to face a penalty shot from Geoff Hurst, who had beaten him on a penalty shot the game before. As soon as Hurst kicked the ball, Gordon guessed correctly and dove to the right. But he nearly dove too far! Still in the air, stretched out full length, he somehow reached up, slapped Hurst's high shot, and knocked it over the goal.

Seven months after his great save, tragedy struck. Gordon was in a car accident and lost his right eye. Despite the injury, he came back and eventually played in the NASL, where he ended his career.

# Pelé (Edson Arantes do Nascimento)

*To Pelé, soccer is "the beautiful game." To those who love the beautiful game, Pelé is the king, the best soccer player of all time.*

**Born**
1940

**Country**
Brazil

**Position**
Forward

BRAZIL

Pelé played a superb all-around game. His ball control was stupendous. He once dribbled from his own penalty area, up field, around six opponents and their goalie, and scored a goal. His passing has never been equaled. He sometimes passed the ball to himself by bouncing it off an opponent! To try and stop him, other teams often put two or even three defenders on him.

Pelé grew up poor, playing barefooted. He used socks stuffed with rags for soccer balls. At age 15, he began playing for Santos, a city on Brazil's coast. A year later he burst onto the international scene with Brazil's 1958 World Cup championship team.

Pelé's first goal is still remembered. With his back to the goal, he took a pass on his thigh, flicked the ball over his shoulder, spun around, and shot the ball into the goal before it hit the ground.

After the 1958 World Cup, European clubs offered Pelé large sums of money to play for them. To keep him playing at home, the Congress of Brazil declared him a national treasure and prohibited him from leaving the country.

Pelé played in four World Cup tournaments. In the 1970 series, he was unbeatable. He scored once and assisted in every other goal in Brazil's 4-1 finals win over Italy.

When Pelé retired in 1974, he had scored 1,216 goals in 1,254 games. His records include 97 goals

Pelé celebrates after winning the 1970 World Cup.

in 110 international games, and 92 "hat tricks" (games in which he scored three or more goals), seven in international games.

Pelé made moves on the field that nobody had ever seen.

Pelé was a hero around the world. He met presidents and kings and the pope. Chinese guards crossed their border with Hong Kong—for which they could have been shot!—just to shake Pelé's hand. During a war in Nigeria, a cease fire was called so that Pelé could visit both sides. Despite all his fame, Pelé remained a humble man, grateful for his talent.

In 1975, Pelé came out of retirement to play with the New York Cosmos of the NASL. After more than two seasons, he retired for good, finishing with 1,280 career goals in 1,363 games.

Nobody has ever played "the beautiful game" better than Pelé.

# Eusebio da Silva Ferreira

**Born**
1942

**Country**
Mozambique

**Position**
Center Forward

*His lightning speed and deadly right foot earned him the name "the Black Panther." He possessed one of the most powerful shots of all time.*

Two soccer greats meet on the field: Eusebio (left) and Pelé (right).

**P**laying for Portugal, Eusebio became the first world-class soccer star from Africa. He twice scored more goals in a season than any other player in Europe, and in 1965, he was European Footballer of the Year. Two years later he scored 42 goals in only 26 league games.

In the 1966 World Cup, Eusebio scored four goals in one game against North Korea. Portugal was losing 0-3 when Eusebio took control. He scored four goals in a row, and then made a pass to set up another. Portugal won 5-3.

Like Pelé, Eusebio grew up poor. His father died when he was five years old. He helped his mother raise the eight Ferreira children. Eusebio actually played his first soccer game while running errands for his mother. He immediately loved the game. For a long time he played barefooted until he found a

Goalkeepers have to give their all to stop Eusebio from scoring.

Eusebio was the top scorer in the 1966 World Cup, but he weeps here after Portugal was eliminated by England.

single soccer boot in a garbage dump. He carried that boot with him everywhere, playing with it in countless street games. When he signed his first professional contract, his bonus was a new pair of soccer shoes.

After playing in Mozambique, Eusebio played for Benfica, a leading team in Portugal. One of his first games for Benfica was against Pelé's team, Santos. Trailing 0-5 with 30 minutes left, Eusebio entered the game. He scored three times before the game ended. Although Benfica lost, Eusebio became famous.

He led Benfica to ten Portuguese championships and the 1962 European Cup. Ten years later,

Eusebio uses his head in the 1966 World Cup.

Eusebio went to America. In 1976, he captained Toronto to the NASL championship. Since then he has played with teams all over the world.

# Franz Beckenbauer

**Born**
1945

**Country**
Germany

**Position**
Attacking Sweeper

He was a confident leader and Germany's captain. He came to be called "Kaiser Franz"— Emperor Franz.

GERMANY

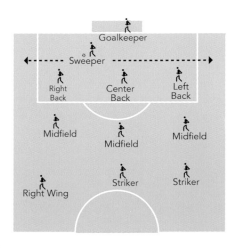

Before Beckenbauer, the sweeper stayed on defense, patrolling the area near the goal.

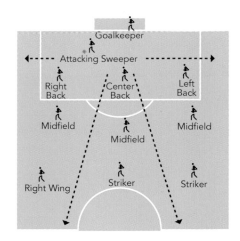

Beckenbauer, the "attacking sweeper," also guarded the goal; but he was free to drive upfield and lead offensive attacks.

F ranz Beckenbauer changed the way soccer is played. In the 1960s in Europe, soccer was a mostly defensive game. The Italians started it, placing a "sweeper" behind their backs to keep the ball away from the goal. Soon every team in Europe was playing with a sweeper, even Franz's team, West Germany.

But Franz added something new. On his German team there were three forwards, three midfielders, and three deep backs. And there was Franz, the "attacking sweeper." Unlike other sweepers, Franz was free to play both in front of and behind his backs. From this position he could see the entire field. When he chose, he could lead offensive attacks. He directed all his teammates. He dominated the entire field.

Franz soon became world famous for his great soccer skill and easy movement. Because he was

a confident leader and Germany's captain, he came to be called "Kaiser Franz"—Emperor Franz.

He led West Germany to the 1972 European Championship and the 1974 World Cup, his third World Cup appearance. His club team, Bayern Munich, won three European Cups in a row (1974–1976). He scored 43 goals in 396 league games, but made many more goals possible with his superb passing. In 1977, like many other European stars, Franz played and starred in the North American Soccer League.

After his playing career ended, Franz was named manager of the West German national team. When his team won the 1990 World Cup, Franz had become only the second person to win a World Cup as a player and a manager.

Beckenbauer (left) tangles in the snow during a 1966 game in Munich, Germany.

# George Best

**Born**
1946

**Country**
Northern Ireland

**Position**
Forward

*He often faked out defenders so badly they'd fall to the ground. He made goals from all over the field.*

IRELAND

George Best was a magician with a soccer ball. His daring dribbling reminded fans of Stanley Matthews. His brilliant ball control, with his head or either foot, was nearly as good as Pelé's. His ability to improvise—to make exciting, unplanned moves—was all his own. So, too, were his long black hair and impish grin.

Born in Belfast, Northern Ireland, George played most of his games for Manchester United, an English club. He soon became known for unbelievable plays. He once ran down half the field, dribbling the ball with his thighs, not his feet. He often faked out defenders so badly they'd fall to the ground. He made goals from all over the field. He actually scored one goal while in a headstand!

In 350 games, he scored 135 goals, helping United win the 1968 European Cup. He was named English Footballer of the Year in 1967 and 1968, and European Footballer of the Year in 1968.

George became as popular as a rock star. At first he enjoyed his fame, but he soon tired of it. He was hounded by photographers wherever he went. Anything he did appeared in the newspapers the next day. He began getting into fights both off and on the field.

Still, he continued to surprise people with his daring antics on the field. He once stood still holding the ball under one foot. He took off his Manchester United shirt. He stood there and waved the red shirt at a defender, as if George were a bullfighter challenging a bull to charge. When the embarrassed defender finally came at him, George waved the shirt and neatly dribbled the ball past him.

By 1972 George had lost much of his magical skills, but he was still good enough to star in the NASL. People who saw George at his best say that no one ever had more ability.

# Diego Maradona

**Born**
1960

**Country**
Argentina

**Position**
Forward

*People expected to see him flying over other players or exploding around a defender in a burst of speed.*

ARGENTINA

In the 1986 World Cup tournament, Maradona scored every goal in Argentina's quarterfinals and semi-finals victories. And when the championship game with Germany was tied 2-2, Maradona made the pass that set up the winning goal. People call the 1986 World Cup "Maradona's Cup."

Like other soccer stars, Diego's natural athletic ability was discovered early in his life. At age 16, he was already playing for Argentina's national team. His short, stocky form and attacking style soon became known all over the world. People expected to see him flying over other players or exploding around a defender in a

burst of speed. Opposing teams began watching and guarding him closely.

Although he appeared for his home country, Argentina, in four World Cup tournaments (1982, 1986, 1990, and 1994), he played most of his games for European clubs. First he played for Barcelona, Spain, scoring 22 goals in only 36 league games. He then went to Napoli, Italy, in 1984. It was the most expensive deal in soccer history. Despite injuries and illness, he continued scoring goals. He led Napoli to several Italian league and European championships.

Diego again led Argentina to the championship game of the World Cup finals in 1990. In 1986, he was unbeatable; but in 1990, he failed to score, and Argentina lost.

Even so, Diego Maradona had earned his place in history. He was the world's best player in the 1980s, and one of the greatest soccer stars of all time.

Maradona (holding trophy) and his happy teammates celebrate
Argentina's 1986 World Cup victory.

# Index

## About the Author

Dale Howard was born and raised in India, where his parents served as missionaries. His love of soccer began in school, when he played center forward and won his school's Best All-Around Athlete award.

After working for twenty years at Open Court Publishing in language arts and curriculum development, he is now managing editor at Meadowbrook Press in Minnesota. He also recently received his Master of Divinity degree from Lutheran Northwestern Theological Seminary in St. Paul, Minnesota.

Mr. Howard is married and has four children.

LIBRARY
TELLURIDE PUBLIC SCHOOLS
TELLURIDE, COLORADO 81435

DISCARD